CHUTNEYS, PICKLES
& SQUA...

(Including <u>OIL FREE &</u>

Rajshri

B.Sc. Home Science
(Dietetics & Public Health Nutrition, Lady Irwin College)

Nita Mehta
Cook with Confidence

CHUTNEYS, SQUASHES & PICKLES

© Copyright 1999-2011 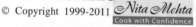 *Nita Mehta* — Cook with Confidence

7th Print 2011

ISBN 978-81-7676-004-1

Illustrations & Editing:  *Nita Mehta* — Cook with Confidence

Layout and Laser Typesetting:

 National Information Technology Academy
3A/3, Asaf Ali Road
New Delhi-110002
☎ 23252948

Published by:

 *Nita Mehta*
Cook with Confidence

3A/3 Asaf Ali Road, New Delhi - 110002
Tel: 91-11-23252948, 91-11-23250091
E-Mail: nitamehta@nitamehta.com
Website: http://www.nitamehta.com

Distributed by :

NITA MEHTA BOOKS — Distributors & Publishers
3A/3, Asaf Ali Road, New Delhi - 02

Distribution Centre:
D16/1, Okhla Industrial Area, Phase-I,
New Delhi-110020
Tel.: 26813199, 26813200

Printed in India

Contributing Writers :
Anurag Mehta
Tanya Mehta
Subhash Mehta

Editors :
Sangeeta
Sunita

 Recipe Development & Testing:
Nita Mehta Foods - R & D Centre
3A/3, Asaf Ali Road, New Delhi-110002
E-143, Amar Colony, Lajpat Nagar-IV
New Delhi-110024

Rs. 89/-

FOREWORD

Pickles and chutneys add variety and zest to meals. They also help in digestion by stimulating the flow of gastric juices.

Preservation of fruits and vegetables at home is done by the use of salt, sugar, vinegar (acid), oil and spices. It can also be done by adding chemical preservatives as sodium benzoate or potassium metabisulphite (KMS), as for squashes. These are easily available with chemists or at grocery shops.

Foods are preserved by the destruction or inactivation of micro-organisms and toxins produced by them which are responsible for the spoilage of food. Oil when used in pickles forms a top layer which prevents the micro-organisms in the air from coming into contact with the food. Vinegar, ensures an acidic medium, which is not favourable for the growth of micro-organisms. Similarly, the presence of high concentration of salt and sugar, draws water from the tissue cells of fruits and vegetables, and thus prevents water from being available for bacterial growth. Spices produce toxic effects on micro-organisms. This is the basis of the various methods employed for preservation.

CONTENTS

Tips for Pickles

1. Fruit or vegetable to be pickled should be fresh and juicy.
2. The vegetables should be dried well before mixing with the masalas. There should be no traces of water clinging to the vegetables.
3. Always use thick bottomed vessels, preferably stainless steel or non stick utensils for preparing pickles.
4. The vessel in which the pickle is to be kept should be clean and dry.
5. Keep the pickle in the sun from time to time till ready.
6. Pickles or chutneys should be taken out in smaller bottles for daily use.
7. If the lid of the pickle bottle is not properly closed, there are chances of getting fungus in the pickle.
8. Do not use a dirty or wet spoon while taking out the pickle from the jar.
9. Oil pickles should be fully covered with oil for longer shelf life. Oil is first heated to smoking point to remove it's odour and then cooled. It is then poured in the jar of pickle till it rises ½" above the masala & floats on top. Mostly mustard oil is used.
10. Normally for 1 kg vegetables, 100 gms salt is used.

Tips for Squashes & Chutneys

1. To sterilize bottles, place clean bottles in a big vessel. Fill the vessel with tap water and boil. Keep the bottles boiling on low flame for 20 minutes to sterilize. Take out the bottles and dry them upside down.
2. Very hot chutneys or squashes, if filled immediately after removing from fire, may crack glass bottles and jars or distort them, if plastic.
3. Do not fill the bottles till the top, always leave 1 to 1½" neck space at the top.
4. Potassium metabisulphite (preservative) should be dissolved in little hot water and then added for even mixing.
5. The preservative is added after removing the chutney or squash from fire.
6. To seal the bottles, melt the wax in a bowl and dip the tightly closed bottle's cover in it fully.
7. If the fruit is very sour, a little extra sugar may be added.
8. If the fruit is slightly discoloured, a little food colour may be added to the squash or chutney to give it a better colour.

TEST FOR CHUTNEYS AND SYRUPS

PLATE TEST FOR CHUTNEYS :

Put a little chutney on a plate, tilt the plate, if the water separates, the chutney is not yet ready. If it remains as a full mass and no water droplet separates, then the chutney is fully cooked.

ONE THREAD CONSISTENCY FOR SYRUPS :

Boiling of sugar and water together for few minutes will give one thread sugar syrup. Do not over boil.

The boiling sugar syrup is sticky, so when a little is put between the thumb and the fore finger and the finger is pulled apart, a small string or thread is formed.

PRACTICAL CONVERSIONS

The ingredients used for making preserves are normally weighed to get good results and to make them last longer without getting spoilt. The oil, sugar, salt and vinegar added to the pickles all help in preserving the pickles and chutneys. Hence the right quantity of these in the recipes is important. It is worth while to invest in a kitchen weighing scale which is easily available at all stores. But for those who do not posses a scale, here are the conversions. All spoons are level. A teaspoon is written as tsp and a tablespoon as tbsp. A teacup is used for the practical conversions.

1 tsp haldi = 5 gm
1 tsp red chilli powder = 5 gm
1 tsp salt = 5 gm
1 tsp garam masala = 5 gm
1 tsp sodium benzoate = 3 gm

1 pod garlic = 25-30 gms
1 medium onion = 75 gms
1½" piece ginger = 35-40 gm
1 cup oil = 175-200 gm
1 cup vinegar = 175-200 ml

TAMATAR KI CHUTNEY

Picture on page 17

1 kg tomatoes
3 tsp red chilli powder
4 tsp salt
30 gms or 1½" piece ginger - grated
30 gms (1 whole pod) garlic - chopped
1 onion - chopped
2 cups sugar
1½ cups vinegar
60 gms (2 tbsp) kishmish (raisins) - cleaned
30 gms (1 tbsp) badaam (almonds) - cut finely
20 (chhoti illaichi) green cardamom - deseeded & powdered

1. Put tomatoes in boiling water for 5 minutes. Remove from water, wipe and remove the skin.
2. Cut tomatoes into small pieces.
3. Chop onion, garlic and grate ginger.
4. Mix tomatoes, garlic, onion and ginger in a clean kadhai. Cook, stirring, till the tomatoes turn soft and thick.
5. Add sugar, salt and vinegar.
6. Add cleaned raisins, almonds and cardamom powder. Cook further for 10 minutes on low flame, till it thickens.
7. Remove from fire. Cool slightly and fill while warm in sterilized bottles. Cover with a lid after it cools.

AAM KI CHUTNEY

Picture on page 36

2 kg raw mangoes - peel and grate to get 1 kg pulp
1 kg sugar
50 gm ginger (2" piece approx.)
70 gm salt
4 to 5 tsp red chilli powder or black pepper powder
3-4 tsp garam masala
1½ tsp acetic acid
1 gm or ¼ tsp sodium benzoate
25 gm magaz or seeds of melons (optional)

1. Wash, peel and grate raw mangoes. Weigh the mango pulp to get 1 kg.
2. Peel and grate ginger.
3. Mix grated mangoes and ginger in a clean kadhai.
4. Cook till the water evaporates.
5. Add sugar to the cooked mangoes and cook further till sugar dissolves and the chutney thickens.
6. Add salt, garam masala and red chilli or pepper powder.
7. Add acetic acid.
8. Remove from fire.
9. Add magaz. Mix.
10. Dissolve sodium benzoate in 1 tsp hot water and add to the chutney.
11. Cool and fill the chutney while still warm in sterilized jars. Cover with the lid after it cools.

ALOO BUKHARA CHUTNEY

250 gm dry aloo bukhara (dried plums) - soaked overnight in 2 cups water
500 gm sugar
3/4 cup lemon juice
3 tsp salt
1-2 tsp black pepper
8 to 10 chhoti illaichi (green cardamoms) - seeds powdered
5 to 6 moti illaichi (black cardamom) - seeds powdered
1 tsp red chilli
100 gm kishmish (raisins)
100 gm badaam (almonds)

GRIND TO A PASTE
1" piece ginger
a small bunch of poodina (fresh mint leaves)

Arbi Pickle : Recipe on page 67 ➢
Tamatar ki Chutney : Recipe on page 12 ➢

1. Soak the dried aloo bukharas in 2 cups water overnight, in a steel bowl.
2. Drain the water. Mash and squeeze the pulp.
3. Wash raisins. Cut chuaras and almonds finely.
4. Grind ginger and pudina together to a paste.
5. To the aloo bukhara pulp, add ginger and pudina paste, sugar and lemon juice. Cook for 5 minutes.
6. Add salt, cardamom, black pepper, almonds and raisins. Cook on low flame till it thickens.
7. Do the plate test (page 10) to see if the chutney is ready. Remove from fire.
8. Cool and fill the chutney while still warm in sterilized jars. Cover with the lid after it cools.

◁ *Amla Pickle : Recipe on page 85*
◁ *Gajar ka Rai waala Achaar : Recipe on page 88*

BANANA & DATE CHUTNEY

1 kg bananas (6 large bananas) - peeled & sliced
1 kg sour apples - peeled, cored and chopped
½ kg dates - stoned and chopped
juice of 2 large oranges
finely grated rind of ½ orange
1 tsp dalchini (cinnamon) powder, a pinch of jaiphal (nutmeg) powder
8-10 laung (clove) - ground, 1 tsp ginger powder
4 tsp salt, black pepper powder to taste
900 ml vinegar
½ kg sugar

1. Place all ingredients in a large thick bottomed pan.
2. Stir over low heat till the sugar dissolves.
3. Bring to a boil, reduce the heat and simmer until the fruit is reduced and the chutney is thick. Spoon into clean, dry jars, seal well.
4. Keep for a day before consuming.

APPLE CHUTNEY - 1

1 kg apple pulp obtained from 1½ kg apples after peeling & grating
500 to 750 gms sugar (depending on the sweetness of the fruit)
3-4 tsp salt
3-4 tsp freshly ground black pepper powder
2 tsp garam masala or 1-2 tsp dalchini (cinnamon) powder
2 tsp acetic acid
¼ tsp sodium benzoate

1. Peel and grate the apples. Weigh to get 1 kg pulp.
2. Add sugar and cook till it thickens.
3. Add salt, pepper & either garam masala or cinnamon powder, according to your taste. Remove from fire after doing the plate test. (see page 10).
4. Add acetic acid.
5. Dissolve sodium benzoate in 1 tsp hot water and mix with the chutney.
6. Fill warm in sterilized jars. Cover with the lid when the chutney cools.

APPLE CHUTNEY - II

1 kg apple slices obtained after peeling & cutting 1½ kg apples approx.
1 kg sugar
5 gm garlic (6-8 flakes) - chopped
50 gm onion (1 small) - chopped
5 gm ginger (½" piece) - grated
3 gm (3/4 tsp) red chilli powder
3 gm (3/4 tsp) black pepper powder
50 gm salt
1½ cups vinegar
¼ tsp sodium benzoate

* WHOLE MASALAS (GRIND TOGETHER)
seeds of 5 gm (3-4) moti illaichi (black cardamoms)
5 gm (1 tsp) laung (cloves)
5 gm (1" stick) dalchini (cinnamon)
5 gm (1 tsp) jeera (cumin seeds)

1. Wash, peel and cut apples. Weigh the slices to get 1 kg.
2. Put the apple slices in 1 litre (5 cups) water to which 1 tsp salt has been added. This prevents the apples slices from getting discoloured
3. Boil water for 2-3 minutes till they are soft. Drain out the water.
4. Cover the slices with sugar. Leave aside and allow to sweat for 1 hour.
5. Tie up all the freshly ground whole masalas, red chilli powder, onion, ginger and garlic, all together in muslin cloth to make a spice bag.
6. Add vinegar to the apple slices.
7. Immerse the spice bag in slices and cook it on slow fire till the desired consistency is obtained.
8. Remove the spice bag, then add salt, pepper and vinegar. Cook it for 5-10 minutes. Do the plate test to see if the chutney is ready (see page 10). Remove from fire.
9. Add sodium benzoate by dissolving in 1 tsp hot water. Fill in clean jars.

NOTE : * If you wish, you may use 2 tsp ready made garam masala instead of grinding fresh whole masalas. Add it after the chutney is ready.

MANGO NAV RATTAN CHUTNEY

2 kg raw mangoes - peeled & grated into thick shreds (lachhas)
500 gms chhuara (dried dates) - deseeded and cut lengthwise
100 gm ginger - peeled & grated
1¼ kg sugar
4-5 tsp kala namak (rock salt), 4 tsp salt
50 gm magaz (melon seeds)
100 gm kishmish (raisins)
100 gms badaam (almonds) - cut finely

SAUTE TOGETHER & GRIND COARSELY (WHOLE SPICES)
1 tsp ghee
seeds of 25 gm moti illaichi (black cardamoms)
1 tsp kesar (saffron), 5 gm (1 tsp) laung (cloves)
5 gm (1 tsp) javitri (mace), 3 gm (½ tsp) jaiphal (nutmeg)
5 gm (1½") dalchini (cinnamon)

1. Saute all the whole spices together in 1 tsp ghee on low flame for 2 minutes. Coarsely grind all the spices together.
2. Cook sugar and 1 cup water to make one thread consistency syrup.
3. Add grated mangoes, ginger and chhuara and cook for 10 minutes on low flame, till the chutney thickens. Put a little on a plate and if the liquid doesn't separate, the chutney is ready.
4. Add the freshly ground spices, salt and black pepper powder.
5. Add magaz (melon seeds), kishmish (raisins) and finely cut badaam (almonds). Remove from fire.
6. Fill slightly hot in sterilized jars. Close the lid after the chutney cools.

KHAJOOR IMLI CHUTNEY

200 gm deseeded imli (tamarind)
200 gm gur (jaggery)
20 khajoor or chhuara (dates)
3/4 tsp salt
½ tsp kala namak (rock salt)
3/4 tsp red chilli powder
a pinch of potassium metabisulphite (KMS)

1. Boil imli and gur in 2 cups of water for 10-15 minutes on low flame. Let it cool.
2. Squeeze and strain the pulp. Keep aside.
3. Deseed the dates and cut them length wise into 4 pieces. If you are using chhuaras, soak them in water for 2 hours to soften, and then deseed and chop them.
4. Add salt, kala namak, red chilli powder and khajoor to the tamarind pulp. Cook for 5 to 10 minutes on low heat.
5. Dissolve KMS. in a tea spoon of hot water and add to it.
6. Cool and preserve in a clean bottle.

NOTE : If you do not want chunks of dates, deseed and boil khajoor with imli. Strain the pulp and use.

IMLI SAUNTH

100 gm imli (tamarind)
100 gm dry sticks of amchoor (dried raw mango)
400 gm gur (jaggery)
1 tbsp jeera (cumin seeds)
20-25 saboot kali mirch (pepper corns)
2" stick dalchini (cinnamon)
10-12 laung (cloves)
seeds of 4 moti illaichi (black cardamom)
1 tsp kala namak (rock salt)
1 tsp salt

1. Soak gur, imli and amchoor together overnight.
2. Boil for 15-20 minutes.
3. Sieve through a strainer.
4. Roast laung, dalchini, moti illaichi & saboot kali mirch. Grind together.
5. Cook the pulp and add all the spices.
6. Add salt and kala namak. Cook till it reaches a sauce like consistency.

NOTE :   The left over imli pulp can be used to prepare delicious jal jeera.
         Add salt, poodina paste and enough water to the imli pulp & strain.

TOMATO KETCHUP

3 kg tomatoes - chopped
100 gm or 1 large onion - chopped
10 gm garlic (1/3 of a whole pod) - chopped
50 gm or 1½" piece ginger - chopped
3-4 tsp salt
200 gms sugar
1-2 tsp red chilli
1-2 tsp garam masala
2 tsp glacial acetic acid
1/3 tsp sodium benzoate

1. Wash tomatoes. Chop tomatoes, onion, ginger and garlic.
2. Cook all together for ½ hour or till tender. Pass through a sieve to get a puree.
3. Add sugar to the puree and cook for 10-15 minutes on low flame.
4. Add the red chilli powder and garam masala. Do the plate test.
5. Add salt when the sauce is cooked to prevent the sauce from turning dark in colour. Remove from fire.
6. Add acetic acid.
7. Add sodium benzoate dissolved in 1 tsp of hot water.
8. Cool slightly and fill the ketchup while still warm in sterilized bottles.

TOMATO PUREE

3 kg tomatoes
¼ tsp sodium benzoate
5 tsp (25 gm) salt
1 tsp acetic acid or vinegar

1. Wash and chop tomatoes roughly and blend to a smooth puree in a mixie. Strain the puree.
2. Cook the puree in a thick bottomed pan or a pressure cooker, till it is reduced to almost half it's original volume.
3. When the desired (sauce like) consistency is obtained, do the plate test. Put in a plate. Water should not run.
4. Add salt and acetic acid. Remove from fire.
5. Add sodium benzoate dissolved in 1 tsp hot water.
6. Cool slightly and fill the puree while warm in sterilized jars.

PICKLES

The pickles have been divided into special sections :

OIL FREE for the calorie conscious

❖

INSTANT for the busy women

❖

UNUSUAL for the people who like to experiment

❖

TRADITIONAL the ever green pickles

Nimboo ka Khatta Mitha Achaar

Picture on back cover

1 kg lemons
600 gms sugar, 200 gms salt
3 tsp garam masala
1 tsp kala namak (rock salt)
2 tsp red chilli powder
2 cups white vinegar

1. Wash and wipe lemons till dry.
2. Slit thinly into round slices, leaving the bottom intact.
3. Place the slit lemons in a clean, dry jar.
4. Put sugar, salt, garam masala, kala namak and red chilli powder.
5. Add vinegar and shake well.
6. Keep aside in the sun for at least 10 to 15 days, till the peel turns soft.

Sweet Date & Ginger Pickle : Recipe on page 76 ➤
Aloo Matar Pickle : Recipe on page 86 ➤

Nimboo ka Mitha Achaar with Ajwain

2½ kg lemons
1¼ kg sugar
500 gm salt
1 tbsp ajwain (thymol seeds)
25 gm (5 tsp) kala namak (rock salt)
1 tbsp garam masala

1. Wash and wipe lemons to dry them.
2. Slit the lemons into 4 pieces, taking care to keep the base intact.
3. Mix sugar, salt, ajwain, kala namak and garam masala together.
4. Fill the slit lemons with this masala.
5. Keep in the sun for 10 days, shaking it well in the evenings when you keep it in.

◄ *Lauki Pickle : Recipe on page 84*
◄ *Aam ki Chutney : Recipe on page 14*

SIMPLE NIMBOO KA ACHAAR

1 kg lemon
½ kg sugar
100 gm salt
100 gm saboot kali mirch (pepper corns) - coarsely ground

1. Wash the lemons, dry them with a clean cloth.
2. Slit the lemons into 4 halves, taking care not to cut till the end.
3. Mix sugar, salt and coarsely ground black pepper.
4. Fill the masala mixture in the slit lemons.
5. Transfer the lemons to a clean jar.
6. Cover the pickle with the left over masala.
7. Keep it in sun for 5-6 days till sugar melts.
8. Shake the jar daily and keep inside in the evenings.
9. This pickle is ready within 15-20 days.

LIME PICKLE IN GUR

1½ kg lemons, 250 gms salt
½ kg gur (jaggery) - crushed

WHOLE MASALAS

4 tsp jeera (cumin seeds), 50 gm saboot kali mirch (pepper corns)
50 gm methi dana (fenugreek seeds), 50 gm saunf (fennel seeds)

1. Soak lemons in water overnight.
2. Next day dry the lemons with a clean muslin cloth.
3. Slit the lemons into 4 pieces, taking care not to cut till the end.
4. Rub in salt and keep them in a jar. Place the jar in the sun for 4 days.
5. After 4 days, dry roast the whole masalas together or roast in a tea spoon of ghee. Grind them coarsely.
6. Add the freshly ground masalas and crushed gur to the lemons.
7. Keep the jar of lemons in the sun for 5-6 days. Shake the jar daily and keep inside in the evenings.

KATHAL IN VINEGAR

1 kg kathal - peeled & cut into 1½" pieces
500 ml vinegar
50 gm salt
50 gm red chilli powder

DRY ROAST TOGETHER AND GRIND ROUGHLY
50 gm saunf (fennel seeds)
50 gm dhania saboot (coriander seeds)

1. Put the kathal in boiling salted water. Boil till kathal turns a little soft. Dry on a muslin cloth.
2. Add the dried kathal to the vinegar.
3. Add the freshly ground saunf and saboot dhania.
4. Add salt and red chilli powder.
5. This pickle is ready in a day for consumption.

Sweet Kathal Pickle

1 kg kathal - peeled and cut into 1½" pieces
200 ml (1 cup) vinegar
250 gm gur (jaggery)
100 gm salt
50 gm dhania powder
50 gm saunf (aniseeds)
50 gm red chilli powder
25 gm ginger powder

1. Boil the kathal in salted water till soft. Dry for 5-6 hours on a muslin cloth.
2. Boil gur and vinegar for about 5 minutes till the gur dissolves completely.
3. Pass it through a sieve or remove the dirt from top with a strainer.
4. To the gur syrup, add salt, dhania powder, saunf, red chilli powder and ginger powder.
5. Add the dried kathal and store in a clean jar.

Khatta Metha Aam ka Achaar

1 kg raw mango slices (take 1.5 kg whole raw mangoes)
100 gm salt, 25 gm red chilli powder
25 gm rai powder
50 gm methi daana (fenugreek seeds)
200 gm sugar

DRY ROAST TOGETHER AND GRIND TO A POWDER
50 gm saunf (fennel seeds)
50 gm saboot dhania (coriander seeds)

1. Peel and cut the mangoes in to 1" slices. Weigh to get 1 kg slices.
2. In a paraat, put the mango slices. Add salt, chilli powder, rai powder, methi daana, sugar and the freshly powdered saunf and dhania.
3. Mix the mango slices with the masalas thoroughly.
4. Fill in a jar and keep in the sun for a week. Keep the pickle inside in the evenings.

MANGO PICKLE WITH LESS OIL

1 kg mangoes - cut into ½" pieces without peeling
100 gm salt
3-4 tsp mustard oil
½ tsp hing, 25 gm kalongi (nigella seeds)
25 gm haldi, 25-50 gm red chilli powder

DRY ROAST & GRIND
50 gm saunf (fennel seeds)
25 gm saboot dhania (coriander seeds)

1. Wash and cut mangoes into ½" cubes. Apply half of the salt and leave it overnight.
2. Dry the mango pieces on a clean cloth for 4-5 hours.
3. Heat oil. Remove from fire. Add hing & kalongi. Add haldi, salt, red chilli powder and freshly roasted & ground saunf and dhania. Mix.
4. Add mangoes and mix well. Store in a clean jar. Keep in the sun for 2-3 days.

MANGO & GINGER JULIENNES

Picture on page 53

1 kg mango - cut into juliennes (long thin pieces)
250 gm ginger - cut into juliennes, 100 gm salt, 250 gm sugar
25 gm (5 tsp) bhuna jeera (roasted cumin seeds)- powdered
50 gm (10 tsp) red chilli powder, 1 tsp kala namak (rock salt)

1. Peel and cut mangoes and ginger into juliennes (long thin pieces).
2. Apply salt to both for 3-4 hours. Drain out the water.
3. Add sugar. Cook for 5-10 minutes on low flame, till it turns soft.
4. Add jeera, red chilli powder and kala namak. Transfer to a sterilized jar and can be consumed instantly.

NOTE : Sugar may be added at the end along with the masala and cooking is then not required. Instead the pickle is kept in the sun for 3-4 days till the sugar dissolves. This uncooked pickle will be crunchier than the cooked one.

GREEN CHILLI PICKLE

Picture on page 53

200 gms (15-20) green chillies (slightly thick ones)
8 tsp rai powder, 1 tsp haldi
3 tsp salt, 8 tsp amchoor
6 tsp mustard oil

1. Wash and wipe green chillies.
2. Slit the chillies and dry in shade for 1-2 hours.
3. Mix all the dry masalas. Mix 1 tsp of oil to them to bind the masalas together.
4. Fill the prepared masala in the chillies.
5. Heat 4 to 5 tsp of oil in a kadhai or a pan. Add the green chillies and saute for 2-3 minutes on low flame till the chillies become slightly soft. Do not let them get discoloured.
6. Fill in sterilized bottles.

LIME RIND PICKLE

1 kg peels of lime - cut into shreds (juice may be used in making squash or hing waala mirch ka achaar - page 48)

1.4 kg sugar

500 ml water

5 gm citric acid

60 gm salt

5 gm (1 tsp) red chilli powder

5 gm (1 tsp) black pepper powder

25 gm ginger (1" piece) - peeled & sliced

10 gm (10-15 flakes) garlic - peeled & sliced

400 ml white vinegar

2 tbsp (kishmish) raisins, ¼ tsp jaiphal (nutmeg), ¼ tsp javitri (mace)

GRIND TOGETHER COARSELY

1" stick dalchini (cinnamon)

8-10 laung (cloves)

seeds of 10 moti illaichi (black cardamom)

1. Extract the lime juice. Keep juice aside.
2. Cut each half peel into 4 pieces to get shreds.
3. Cook rind shreds in boiling water containing a pinch of soda bicarb for 5-10 minutes. Drain out the water.
4. Mix sugar with 500 ml water and citric acid. Boil to get a sugar syrup.
5. Strain the syrup through a muslin cloth.
6. Coarsely grind the cinnamon, cardamom and cloves.
7. Mix lemon shreds in syrup and add all the spices.
8. Add only half of the vinegar. Cook on slow fire, till the syrup becomes thick and the shreds appear transparent.
9. Add the left over vinegar. Remove from fire and fill in a clean jar.

HING WAALA MIRCH KA ACHAAR

1 kg chillies - thick variety
100 gm rai powder
25 gm kala namak (rock salt)
150 gm salt
250 gm ginger
juice of 15-20 lemons
5 gm (3/4 tsp) hing (asafoetida)
½ cup mustard oil

DRY ROAST & COARSELY GRIND
100 gm saunf (fennel seeds)
100 gm saboot dhania (coriander seeds)
100 gm methi dana (fenugreek seeds)

1. Clean green chillies with damp cloth. Slit longitudinally.
2. Heat ½ cup oil to smoking point. Remove from fire. Add hing.
3. Add rai, kala namak and salt.
4. Add the freshly ground masalas.
5. Fill the ready masala into the slit mirchis. Put them in jar. Keep the jar in the sun for 1 day.
6. Next day, cut ginger into juliennes or match sticks. Apply 2 tsp salt to it.
7. Add this ginger to stuffed chillies.
8. Taking care to remove seeds, squeeze lemon juice such that it covers the achaar nicely. (This will make it last longer.)

BHARWAAN MIRCH

1 kg green chillies of thick variety
125 gms saunf (fennel seeds)
100 gm amchoor, 25 gm haldi, 100 gm rai powder (mustard powder)
125 gm or slightly more than ½ cup salt
3/4 cup (½ cup and ¼ cup) mustard oil

1. Wipe the green chillies with a damp cloth.
2. Slightly roast the saunf on tawa and coarsely grind it.
3. Slit chillies, remove seeds, smear the chillies with ¼ cup mustard oil.
4. Heat ½ cup oil to smoking point. Remove from fire and cool it.
5. Add saunf, rai powder, salt and amchoor. Mix well.
6. Fill this masala into the chillies.
7. Keep it in the sun for a week. Keep shaking and mixing the pickle daily.

NOTE : For a longer shelf life, heat 1 cup mustard oil to smoking point. Cool and add to the pickle after it is ready.

GAL GAL KA ACHAAR

1 kg gal gal
250 gm ginger - cut into match sticks
100 gms whole dry, red chillies
150 gm salt
50 gm red chilli powder, 3-4 tsp haldi
1½ -2 cups mustard oil (enough to soak achaar)

1. Wash and wipe gal gal with a clean muslin cloth. Cut into 1" pieces.
2. Transfer to a jar. Add salt and keep in the sun for 2-3 days, till the colour of the gal gal peel changes slightly.
3. Cut ginger. Add to the gal gal in the jar.
4. Heat oil to smoking point. Remove from fire. Add broken red chilli bits.
5. Add haldi and red chilli powder. Add to the gal gals.

NOTE :   Kabuli channa soaked overnight and dried can also be added to the above pickle.

GAJAR, GOBHI, SHALGAM KA ACHAAR

Picture on page 54

2.5 kg (all 3 vegetables mixed together)
100 gm garlic - ground to a paste, 100 gm ginger - ground to a paste
100 gm salt , 100 gm rai powder
4-5 tsp haldi, 100 gms red chillies (for a hot pickle, add more chillies)
500 gm gur (jaggery)
2 cups (500 ml) vinegar
500 gm mustard oil
25 gm kasuri methi (dried fenugreek leaves)

1. Peel carrots and shalgam (turnips). Cut carrots into fingers, shalgam into round slices and cauliflower into medium sized florets.
2. Boil water in a big pan. Add vegetables. Remove from fire. Keep aside in the hot water for ½ hour.

Green Chilli Pickle : Recipe on page 45 ➤
Mango & Ginger Juliennes : Recipe on page 44 ➤

3. After half an hour remove the vegetables from the water with a slotted spoon and dry them on a clean cloth in the shade.
4. Next day, heat oil to smoking point, reduce flame. Add garlic paste and fry till light golden in colour.
5. Add ginger paste and fry till light brown. Remove from fire.
6. Add salt, rai powder, kasuri methi, red chilli powder and haldi to the ginger-garlic mixture.
7. Smear the dried vegetables with this masala and put them in a jar.
8. In a pan heat vinegar, add gur to it and cook till gur dissolves. Strain it, cool and add it to the pickle in the jar. Shake well so that it mixes evenly with the vegetables.
9. Keep in the sun for 4-5 days.

NOTE : If you want the pickle to be sweet, reduce the chilli and increase the gur according to taste.
If you like the pickle to be soft, boil the vegetables for 2-3 minutes and then remove from fire.

◄ *Gajar, Gobhi, Shalgam ka Achaar : Recipe on page 52*

KATHAL PICKLE

1 kg kathal - cut into 1½" pieces
150 gm salt
2 cups mustard oil - approx.
50 gm rai powder (mustard powder)
50 gm dhania powder (coriander powder)
50 gm haldi
50 gm red chilli
25 gm methi daana (fenugreek seeds) - dry roast lightly on a tawa
50 gm saunf (fennel seeds) - dry roast lightly on a tawa
2-3 tsp kalonji (nigella seeds)
4-6 tsp amchoor

1. Boil the kathal with 2 tsp salt till soft. Drain the water and dry it on muslin cloth for 5-6 hours.
2. Heat 1 cup oil in a karahi to smoking point. Remove from fire.
3. Add salt, rai powder, dhania powder, haldi, red chilli, methi daana, saunf, kalonji and amchoor. Mix.
4. Rub the kathal with this masala and put it in a jar.
5. Next day, heat about 1 cup mustard oil to smoking point. Remove from fire and cool the oil.
6. Pour this oil in the jar of pickle, adding enough oil to cover the kathal properly.
7. Keep the achaar in the sun for 4-5 days. Keep shaking the jar daily.

SABOOT MANGO PICKLE (GUJARATI STYLE)

A slightly sweet pickle of small whole mangoes.

1 kg raw mangoes - small sized
25 gm haldi
200 gm salt
400 gm or 2 cups mustard oil or til (sesame seeds) oil
50 gm methi daana (fenugreek seeds)
½ tsp hing (asafoetida)
25 gm rai powder (mustard powder)
25 gm red chilli powder
100 gm sugar - powdered

1. Wash and slit the mangoes into four, keeping the base intact. Remove the seed, taking care to keep the mangoes whole.
2. Apply half of the salt and half of the haldi. Place them in a jar. Keep in the sun for 2 days.
3. Remove the mangoes from the jar and dry for 5-6 hours.
4. Heat oil to smoking point. Remove from fire. Add hing.
5. Add the left over haldi and salt, methi daana, rai powder, red chilli powder and sugar.
6. Fill the mangoes with this masala.
7. Keep in the sun for 2-3 days.

NOTE : To the left over mango water with haldi and salt, left in the jar from step 3, add a little gur, chhuara, kishmish, badaam, garam masala, black pepper and amchoor. Keep in the sun for 2-3 days. Khatti meethi chutney is ready. Consume within a few days.

MANGO PICKLE (MAHARASHTRIAN)

1 kg raw mangoes
250 gm mustard oil
½ tsp hing
1 large pod or 50 gm garlic - chopped finely
150 gm salt
50 gm red chilli powder, 25 gm haldi
25 gm methi daana - dry roast on a tawa & grind to a powder

1. Cut the mangoes into small pieces. Remove the seed.
2. Heat ½ of the oil, add hing and garlic.
3. Add salt, red chilli powder, haldi and roasted methi daana powder.
4. Cool the masala and add mangoes.
5. Mix it and fill in a jar. Keep in the sun for 2 days.
6. Heat the rest of the oil to smoking point. Cool it and add to the pickle in the jar.
7. Keep the pickle in the sun, shaking the jar daily once.

Adrak aur Gal Gal ka Achaar

1 kg gal gal
50 gm mustard oil
250 gm ginger
100 gm whole, dry red chillies - broken into pieces
250 gm salt
30 gms or 5 to 6 tsp red chilli powder
3 tsp haldi

1. Wash and cut the gal gal into ½" pieces.
2. Cut the ginger into 1" long strips (juliennes).
3. Heat oil to smoking point. Add the whole red chillies.
4. Fill the gal gal, ginger along with salt, red chillies and haldi in jar.
5. Add the oil with the red chillies to it and shake well to mix.
6. To preserve the pickle for a longer time, heat some more oil to smoking point. Cool the oil and pour into the jar of pickle such that it covers the gal gal completely.

TAMATAR KA ACHAAR

1 kg tomatoes
2 tsp haldi (optional)
50 gm garlic - chopped finely
25 gms ginger - chopped finely
2 tsp red chilli powder
4 whole, dry red chillies
1 cup vinegar
125 gm or 1 cup sugar
1 cup mustard oil or cooking oil
50 gm salt

DRY ROAST & GRIND COARSELY
50 gm jeera (cumin seeds)
25 gm methi daana (fenugreek seeds)

1. Clean tomatoes and cut into small pieces.
2. Chop garlic and ginger finely.
3. Dry roast jeera and methi seeds and grind coarsely.
4. Heat oil, add garlic and ginger and fry till light brown.
5. Break red chillies into 3-4 pieces and add to garlic and ginger. Fry for a few seconds.
6. Add chopped tomatoes and cook till tender. Keep stirring constantly.
7. Add sugar and cook till it dissolves.
8. Add vinegar, salt, haldi, freshly ground methi & jeera. Cook for 5 minutes.
9. Remove from fire. Cool and fill in a clean jar.

STUFFED RED CHILLI PICKLE

Picture on page 71

½ kg big red chillies
30 gms (6 tsp) methi seeds – roasted and ground
30 gm (6 tsp) red chilli powder, 50 gm amchoor
100 gm saunf (fennel seeds) – roasted & ground coarsely
100 gm salt, 6 tsp garam masala, 50 gm rai powder (mustard powder)
50 gm jeera powder (cumin powder) - roasted & ground coarsely
4 lemons, 2 cups oil

1. Remove the stem of the chillies and then the seeds from the stem side with the back of a hair pin.
2. Then wet all the ingredients with lemon juice and 4-5 tsp oil which has been heated and cooled.
3. Fill in the masala tightly in the chillies and pack them in a jar. Heat the left over oil to smoking point. Cool it & pour over the chillies.
4. Keep the pickle for one week. Shake the jar carefully every day.

UNPEELED MANGO PICKLE

1.5 kg raw mangoes
150 gm salt
50 gms red chillies powder, 25 gms haldi powder
50 gms saunf (aniseeds) - dry roast lightly
50 gms methi dana (fenugreek seeds), 30 gms kalongi (nigella seeds)
2 cups mustard oil

1. Wash mangoes. Wipe with a clean cloth. Cut into 1" pieces.
2. Heat the oil in a karahi. Cool the oil.
3. Mix salt, red chilli powder, haldi, saunf, methi daana, kalonji and black pepper powder with the oil.
4. Add the mango slices to the masala oil. Mix well.
5. Fill into a jar. Keep jar in the sun, shaking it once daily.
6. To preserve the pickle for a longer time, heat some more oil and cool it.
7. Pour it in the jar of pickle to cover the mango slices.

KACHALU KA ACHAAR

1 kg kachalu
100 gm saunf (fennel seeds)
100 gm salt
100 gm rai powder
100 gm methi daana (fenugreek seeds)
2 tsp haldi, 4 to 6 tsp red chilli powder
250 gm mustard oil
1 cup vinegar

1. Boil the whole kachalu for 10 minutes till it feels soft when a knife is inserted into it.
2. Peel and cut into medium sized pieces and dry on a muslin cloth in the shade.
3. Heat oil. Cool it. Add all the masalas and mix kachaalu pieces with it.
4. Boil vinegar. Cool it and add to the pickle.
5. Keep in the sun for 5-6 days.

ARBI PICKLE

Picture on page 17

½ kg arbi
2 tsp methi seeds (fenugreek seeds), 4 tsp saunf (fennel seeds)
2 tsp garam masala, 3 tsp red chilli powder, 4 tsp salt
1 cup vinegar, 1 cup mustard oil

1. Boil arbi in salted water till almost tender.
2. Peel the arbi and cut it vertically in 2 pieces.
3. Dry roast methi seeds and saunf. Coarsely grind both the spices.
4. Heat oil to smoking point. Fry the arbi and remove from oil.
5. Remove the oil from fire. Add methi, saunf, salt, red chilli, garam masala.
6. Add vinegar and the fried arbi also to it. Keep on fire for 3 to 4 minutes.
7. Cool it and fill in a clean dry jar.

NOTE : This pickle can be kept for 2 weeks in summers & 4 weeks in winters
at room temp. Good for carrying with paranthas on long train journeys.

SWEET MUSHROOM PICKLE

Picture on back cover

½ kg mushroom
50 gm (1 large pod) garlic - ground to a paste
50 gm (2" piece) ginger - ground to a paste
1 cup cooking oil
a pinch of hing
4-6 tsp red chilli powder
5 tsp rai powder
5 tsp salt
½ cup kishmish (raisins)

GRIND TOGETHER
2 tsp methi daana (fenugreek seeds)
2 tsp til (sesame seeds)

BOIL TOGETHER
1 cup vinegar, 1½" piece gur (jaggery)

1. Boil 4-5 cups water with 2 tsp salt. Add mushrooms and boil for about 5 minutes till a little soft. Drain and dry on muslin cloth for 5-6 hours.
2. Heat oil in a kadhai. Fry the garlic paste till light golden, then add ginger and fry till golden brown.
3. Add hing.
4. Add the ground til and methi daana. Remove from fire.
5. Add red chilli powder, rai and salt .
6. Mix the mushroom with this masala.
7. In a pan heat vinegar. Add gur and cook on low flame till gur dissolves.
8. Remove from fire and add kishmish.
9. Add to the mushrooms.
10. Mix well. Put in a jar. Consume within 2 weeks.

KARELA PICKLE

1 kg karela
250 gm raw mango - grated or cut into small bits
50 gm kalonji (nigella seeds)
50 gm red chilli powder
100 gm rai powder
100 gm salt
250 gm kabuli channa
1½ cup mustard oil

ROAST & GRIND COARSELY
50 gm saboot dhania (coriander seeds)
50 gm saunf (fennel seeds)

Amla Pickle : Recipe on page 85 ➢
Stuffed Red Chilli Pickle : Recipe on page 64 ➢

1. Soak the kabuli channas overnight. Drain and dry on a muslin cloth.
2. Peel the karela. Rub half the salt and keep aside for 1 hour. Boil the karelas till soft.
3. Squeeze and dry the karelas in the sun.
4. Grate the raw mangoes or cut very finely after removing the peel.
5. Heat ¼ cup oil. Cool. Add kalonji, red chilli powder, rai powder, crushed saunf and dhania, remaining salt, 50 gm grated raw mangoes and kabuli channa.
6. Fill the masala in karelas and tie with a thread. Transfer to a jar.
7. Keep the jar in the sun for 2-3 days.
8. After 2-3 days, heat the left over oil. Cool it and add to the karelas. Keep in the sun for 1-2 days.

NOTE :   If raw mangoes are not available, add 50 gm amchoor in place of raw mangoes.

◁ *Kesar Illaichi Sherbet : Recipe on page 95*
◁ *Badaam Sherbet : Recipe on page 94*

BRINJAL PICKLE

1 kg brinjal (long thin variety) - cut into 3/4" pieces
½ cup mustard oil
1½ cups vinegar
50 gm salt
50 gm ginger
50 to 100 gm garlic
50 gm (8 tsp) rai powder
2 tsp haldi
2 tsp red chilli powder
50 - 100 gm gur (jaggery) - crushed

ROAST & GRIND
3 tsp jeera (cumin seeds)
3 tsp methi dana (fenugreek seeds)

1. Cut the brinjals into ½" cubes.
2. Heat oil in a karahi and fry the garlic & ginger pastes till golden brown. Remove from fire.
3. Mix rai powder, haldi, red chilli powder, jeera and methi daana to the ginger garlic paste.
4. In a separate vessel dissolve the gur in vinegar by heating on low flame. Remove from fire and keep aside.
5. Add the brinjals and salt to the ginger garlic mixture. Cook for 5 minutes till brinjals are half done.
6. Add the gur & vinegar mixture to the brinjals & cook further for 1 minute.
7. Remove from fire. Cool and fill in a clean jar.

SWEET DATE & GINGER PICKLE

Picture on page 35

1 litre lime juice
80 gms salt
1 kg dry dates (chhuara)
350 gms ginger - peeled & cut into 1" thin strips
1 kg sugar
250 gms kishmish (raisins)
50 gm almonds - finely shredded

FRESHLY GROUND WHOLE MASALAS

25 gms saboot kali mirch (peppercorns) - powdered
25 gms jeera (cumin seeds) - powdered
25 gms moti illaichi (black cardamoms) - powdered
10 gms laung (cloves) - powdered

1. Soak chhuaras (dry dates) overnight in lime juice and salt.
2. Next morning cut the dates and deseed.
3. Peel and cut ginger into 1" thin strips and dry in the sun on a cloth for 3-4 hours.
4. Add sugar, raisins, badaam and ginger to the dates. Allow to stand for 24 hours.
5. In a thick bottomed pan boil the dates in lime juice and simmer for 5 minutes on low flame.
6. Add the powdered pepper corns, cumin seeds, cardamoms and cloves (freshly ground whole masalas) to the boiling mixture and stir well.
7. After a minute remove from the fire and cool.
8. Bottle and use after a week.

STRAWBERRY PICKLE

500 gms strawberries - cleaned, cut into pieces and dried with a cloth
250 gms chhuaras (dry dates) - deseeded and cut lengthwise
220 ml chilli oil
15 gms rai (mustard seeds) - roasted and ground
15 gms methi daana (fenugreek seeds) - roasted and ground
80 gms salt
10 gms saunf (aniseeds)
10 gms black jeera
4 Kashmiri chillies - fried and cut into juliennes
100 gms kishmish (raisins) - fried
50 gms badaam (almonds) - sliced and fried

BOIL TOGETHER
juice of 5 lemons
750 gms sugar

1. Dissolve sugar in lime juice and boil.
2. Add dates and strawberries, and cook thoroughly till it becomes thick and dry.
3. Heat the chilli oil and pour it over this date and strawberry mixture.
4. Add ground mustard seeds, fenugreek seeds, salt, saunf and black jeera.
5. Add fried almonds, raisins and Kashmiri chillies.
6. Mix and store in airtight containers.

CAPSICUM PICKLE

1 kg capsicums - halved or quartered
½ cup mustard oil
a few curry leaves
200 gms sugar
salt to taste

GRIND TO A PASTE
4 tsp jeera (cumin seeds)
2 tsp haldi powder
2 tsp rai (mustard seeds)
2 tsp methi seeds (fenugreek seeds)
50 gms ginger
50 gms garlic
vinegar - enough to grind

1. Heat oil and fry ground paste well.
2. Add the curry leaves.
3. Add capsicums and fry well.
4. Add sugar and salt. Cook on a low flame till done.
5. Remove from fire, cool and bottle.

MANGO INSTANT PICKLE

1½ kg raw mangoes - peeled & cut into thin long pieces
150 gm salt
100 gm (½ cup) mustard oil
a pinch of hing
25 gm (4 tsp) haldi
50 gm saunf (fennel seed) - slightly roasted
50 gm jeera (cumin seeds) - slightly roasted
50 gm red chilli powder

1. Peel and cut mangoes into thin long pieces. Apply salt and keep aside for 2-3 hours.
2. Drain the water from the mango pieces.
3. Heat oil to smoking point. Cool the oil. Add hing, haldi, saunf, jeera and red chilli powder.
4. Add the mango pieces also.
5. Keep it in the sun for a day to be ready for use.

GARLIC PICKLE

½ kg garlic - peeled
(100 gm) ½ cup mustard oil
½ cup vinegar
25 gm (5 tsp) salt
2 tsp haldi
4 tsp red chilli powder
4 tsp rai powder

1. Peel the garlic.
2. Heat mustard oil to smoking point. Reduce flame. Add all the garlic together. Cook for 2 minutes on low flame. Let it cool.
3. Heat vinegar in a separate pan. Remove from fire.
4. Add salt, haldi, red chilli powder and rai powder.
5. Mix the garlic in oil to the masalas in vinegar.
6. Fill it in dry bottles.
7. This pickle can be eaten immediately also.

LAUKI PICKLE

Picture on page 36

1 kg ghiya (bottle gourd) - peeled and cut into fingers
50 gm salt, 3 tsp haldi
3 to 4 tsp red chilli powder, 4 tsp rai powder
½ cup mustard oil, ½ cup or 3/4 cup vinegar

1. Cut ghiya into long fingers.
2. Boil water. Add ghiya. Boil for about 2 min. Remove from fire when ghiya is half done. Remove ghiya from water. Dry on a clean cloth.
3. Heat oil to smoking point. Remove from fire. Add salt, haldi, red chilli powder.
4. Add ghiya and vinegar also. The pickle is ready to eat. Consume within 2 weeks.

NOTE : The quantity of chillies and vinegar can be slightly increased or decreased according to taste.

AMLA PICKLE

Picture on page 18, 71

½ kg amla
150 gm salt
2 tsp jeera (cumin seeds)
2 tsp saunf (fennel seeds)
1-2 tsp methi dana (fenugreek seeds)
1-2 tsp red chilli powder, 1-2 tsp haldi
½ cup mustard oil

1. Boil the amlas in water for 5 minutes. Remove from water.
2. Apply 100 gms salt. Keep aside for 5-6 hours for the water to drain out.
3. Deseed the amlas and cut into half or leave them whole.
4. Heat oil. Shut off the gas. Add jeera, saunf, methi daana, red chilli powder, haldi and 50 gms salt.
5. Add the drained amlas. Cook for 1-2 minutes. Cool. The pickle is ready for use the next day. Consume within 2 weeks.

ALOO MATAR PICKLE

Picture on page 35

1 kg small potatoes - boiled and peeled & dried
500 gm peas - shelled & boiled & dried
50 gm ginger - ground to a paste
50 gm garlic - ground to a paste
1½ cups vinegar
50 gm rai powder
80 gm salt
25 to 50 gm red chilli
25 gm haldi
2-3 tsp kasuri methi (dry fenugreek leaves)
1 cup mustard oil

1. Boil or microwave the potatoes and peas separately. Peel potatoes. Spread on a tray so that the extra water dries up.
2. Mix the rai powder, salt, haldi, red chilli powder and kasuri methi with vinegar.
3. Heat oil. Add garlic paste and fry till it turns light golden.
4. Add ginger paste and fry till light brown.
5. Add the vinegar with the spices to the ginger and garlic paste. Mix well.
6. Add the peas and potatoes. Cook further for a minute. Mix well and remove from fire.
7. Cool and fill in a clean jar. Ready for use in a day or two.

NOTE : This pickle should be consumed within a week.

GAJAR KA RAI WAALA ACHAAR

Picture on page 18

½ kg carrots - peeled and cut into thin 1½" fingers
½ cup vinegar
3 tsp salt
2 tsp red chilli powder
2 tsp haldi
2 tsp rai powder

1. Add carrot pieces to boiling water and keep on fire for 2 minutes.
2. Remove from water and dry for 1-2 hours on a muslin cloth.
3. Apply salt, red chilli powder, haldi and rai powder to the carrots.
4. Transfer the carrot pieces to a jar.
5. Add vinegar to the carrots and shake well to mix. The pickle is ready to eat in a day.

HOT MANGO INSTANT PICKLE

½ kg mangoes - peeled and cut into thin strips
½ tsp hing powder (asafoetida)
100 gm red chilli powder
50 gm salt

1. Peel mangoes. Cut finely into thin strips (lachhas).
2. Mix hing powder, salt and red chilli powder with the mangoes.
3. The pickle is ready to be eaten the next day.

ONIONS IN VINEGAR

12-15 small onions
1 cup white vinegar
1 tsp salt
2 whole, dry red chillies
3-4 laung (cloves)

1. Peel onions. Rub salt and red chilli powder. Keep aside for ½ an hour.
2. Pack the onions, laung and dry red chillies in a jar.
3. Boil vinegar and pour over the onions.

NOTE : 1" piece ginger cut into match sticks may also be added along with onions.

SQUASHES
&
SHERBETS

LITCHI SQUASH

1 litre (5 cups) litchi juice
1.25 kg sugar, 750 ml water
10 gm citric acid, 2 gm (¼ tsp) potassium metabisulphite

1. Wash and peel the fruits and remove seeds.
2. Extract juice in a juicer or a mixer and strain it.
3. Heat water, sugar and citric acid and let it boil.
4. Remove from fire. Sieve the syrup through a muslin cloth to remove scum.
5. Cool it and mix it in the juice.
6. Add potassium metabisulphite after dissolving it in about 1 tsp water.
7. Fill the squash in the sterilized bottles and cap them tightly leaving one inch neck empty. Store in a cool dry place.

SHERBET KHUS

600 gm sugar
480 ml (2½ cups) water
1 tsp khus essence
1 tsp green colouring

1. Prepare syrup with 680 gm sugar and 480 ml water.
2. Boil it to one-thread consistency (see page 10). Do not over boil.
3. Remove from fire and cool.
4. Add essence and colouring.
5. Pour into sterilized bottles.

BADAAM SHERBET

Picture on page 72

150 gm badaam (almonds), 60 gm khus khus (poppy seeds)
2 kg sugar, 1.5 litre (7½ cups) water, 1 tsp citric acid
seeds of 15-20 chhoti illaichi (green cardamom) - powdered
4-5 drops kewra essence, 3 gm (½ tsp) potassium metabisulphite

1. Soak badaam and khus khus separately overnight. Soak khus khus for 2 days, changing the water after the first day.
2. Drain water. Grind badam & khus khus separately to a very fine paste.
3. Boil together sugar and water to make sugar syrup. Add citric acid. Remove the scum (dirt) with a strainer.
4. Add khus and cardamom to syrup. Boil. Remove from fire. Sieve through a muslin cloth.
5. Add badaam paste and essence to the above syrup.
6. Dissolve potassium metabisulphite in a tsp of hot water. Add to the sherbet and mix well. Fill in sterilized bottles.

KESAR ILLAICHI SHERBET

Picture on page 72

2 kg sugar, 1.5 litres (7½ cups) water
2 tsp kesar - soak in ½ cup water
seeds of 20-30 chhoti illaichi (green cardamom) - powdered
a pinch of dry yellow colour or 5-6 drops of liquid yellow colour
½ tsp level potassium metabisulphite

1. Soak kesar in ½ cup water for 2 hours.
2. Boil together sugar and water to make sugar syrup.
3. If the sugar syrup is dirty, clean the sugar syrup by straining through a fine muslin cloth. Cool.
4. Add yellow colour, kesar and powdered cardamom to the cooled syrup.
5. Dissolve potassium metabisulphite in a tsp of hot water and mix it with the syrup. Fill in sterilized bottles.

LEMON GINGER ALE

3/4 cup lime juice, ¼ cup ginger juice
2 cups sugar, 1 cup water
¼ tsp potassium metabisulphite

1. Prepare sugar syrup by boiling sugar and water. Give just 2-3 boils.
2. Strain through a muslin cloth. Cool the sugar syrup.
3. Wash the limes, cut into halves and extract the juice.
4. Peel the ginger. Extract juice through a juicer or grate and extract the juice by squeezing through a muslin cloth.
5. Mix both the juices.
6. Mix the juices with the cooled sugar syrup.
7. Dissolve potassium metabisulphite in 1 tsp of hot water and add to the squash. Fill in sterilized bottles.

MANGO SQUASH

600 gm mango pulp of Dussehri mangoes (1 kg mangoes)
1.5 kg sugar
1.5 kg (7½ cups) water
30 gm citric acid
½ tsp potassium metabisulphite

1. Boil sugar and water together to make sugar syrup. Add citric acid.
2. Remove the scum (dirt) which comes to the surface. Remove from fire and strain the syrup.
3. Mix potassium metabisulphite in a tsp of water and add to the syrup. Keep aside to cool.
4. Extract pulp from mangoes.
5. Add the mango pulp to the syrup when it becomes cool.
6. Fill in sterilized bottles.

FALSA SQUASH

1 kg falsa
2½ kg sugar
3 + 3 (6) cups water
3 tsp citric acid
½ tsp sodium benzoate

1. Wash the falsas. Boil in 3 cups water for 15 minutes.
2. Squeeze the pulp through a clean muslin cloth or sieve.
3. Add 3 cups of water to sugar and keep it to boil. Add citric acid to it on boiling.
4. Sieve the syrup through muslin cloth, cool and mix with falsa juice.
5. Dissolve soda benzoate in one tsp water and add to it.
6. Fill in sterlized bottles.

ORANGE SQUASH

1.5 kg sugar
1 litre (5 cups) water
3 cups orange juice
4 to 5 tsp citric acid
½ tsp potassium metabisulphite
a pinch of orange colour
orange essence - optional

1. Squeeze the orange juice. Immediately add potassium metabisulphite, other wise the juice becomes bitter.
2. Make sugar syrup by boiling water and sugar.
3. Add citric acid. Boil for 4-5 minutes. Remove from fire. Strain to remove the dirt.
4. Cool the sugar syrup.
5. Add orange colour & essence.
7. Add the orange juice to syrup. Fill in sterilized bottles.

NIMBOO KA SHERBET

600 gms sugar
1 kg lemon

1. Fill a clean bottle with sugar.
2. Squeeze juice from lemons.
3. Add the lemon juice to the sugar in bottle.
4. Keep the sharbat in the sun for 10 days. Keep shaking the bottle daily.
   (The sugar will dissolve in the lemon juice by keeping in the sun).

NOTE :   This squash can last for a year, although no preservative is added.

To Use Lemon Peel for sweet lemon pickle :
Cut the peel into shreds. Add salt, garam masala, sugar & vinegar. You may add a little lemon juice also.

APPLE JUICE CONCENTRATE

1 kg apples - cut and peeled
1 kg sugar
2 tsp citric acid
3 cups water
½ tsp potassium metabisulphite

1. Peel and cut the apples and put in 3 cups water.
2. Add sugar and citric acid. Cook till apples become tender.
3. Mix in a blender or pass through a sieve.
4. Add the potassium metabisulphite (preservative) to the hot pulp and preserve in bottles.
5. Dilute according to taste.

Plum Juice Concentrate

1 kg plum
1 kg sugar
2½ to 3 cups water
1½ tsp citric acid
½ tsp potassium metabisulphite

1. Wash plums. Add water to them and keep it to boil for about 15 minutes on low flame till the seeds get separated.
2. Add sugar and cook till it dissolves.
3. Add citric acid to it and cook for a minute.
4. Sieve through a strainer.
5. Heat it and add potassium metabisulphite dissolved in a tsp of hot water to it. Pour in sterilized bottles.
6. To make a drink, add 2 parts water to one part concentrate.
7. A pinch of rock salt (kala namak) can also be added.

Lime Juice Cordial

12 lemons (ripe, good lemons)
400 gm sugar
1 litre water
¼ tsp potassium metabisulphite

1. Cut the lemons into four pieces. Remove seeds. In a pan, boil lemons with 1 litre water and sugar.
2. Simmer for 5 minutes till lemons are soft.
3. Remove from fire.
4. Strain through a muslin cloth and squeeze the lemon juice also through the muslin.
5. Add potassium metabisulphite dissolved in 1 tsp hot water to the lime juice cordial.
6. Preserve in sterilized bottles.

BEST SELLERS BY

Biryanis & Pulaos

Baking Recipes

Baby Cookbook

Microwave Cakes & Snacks

Diet Snacks & Desserts

Drinks & Indian Desserts

Indian Favourites Vegetarian

Lebanese Recipes

Pasta Recipes Vegetarian

Sandwiches & Wraps

Paranthas & Rice for Kids

Recipes for Growing Kids